LOST.

By Wendy Body

Contents

Longman

4

Where Do All the Lost Gloves Go?

Where do all the lost gloves go?

That's the thing I want to know.

Do they hide up in the trees?

Do they fly round in the breeze?

Do rabbits take them for their beds?

Do squirrels wear them on their heads?

Do frogs and toads take them for boats?

Do hedgehogs wear them for their coats?

Or do they run to far off lands
to the monster with a million hands?

19

That's it!

All the gloves that are lost and old
go to keep the monster warm when it's cold!

My Family

My family is great …
great at losing things!

Grandad lost his hair
when he got very old.

Auntie lost her voice
when she caught a cold.

Mum lost her temper
when she dropped a jar.

Dad lost his way
when he was in the car.

The cat lost some fur
when she had a fight.

My team lost the game
when we played last night.

My sister lost the race
when she dropped the egg.

My brother lost his heart
when he fell in love with Meg.

I lost my teacher
when she left our school.

And Gran lost her teeth
when she jumped in the pool!